Review of Mark Levin's

The Democrat Party Hates America

The Democrat Party is now a Marxist party whose goal is to destroy America

---

Book Review by Former State Representative

Gary Giordano (R-AZ, 1985–1989

Executive Director, White House Watch

Introduction by State Representative Mike Jones

(R–York County PA)

Review of Mark Levin's *The Democrat Party Hates America; The Democrat Party is now a Marxist party whose goal is to destroy America* is published by Freedom Publishers Inc. (FreedomPublishers.com) for White House Watch (WhiteHouse.Watch).

This is a Review, not the full book. Freedom Publishers is not associated with Mark Levin or the publisher of his book, which we recommend.

Book Review by Former Arizona State Representative Gary Giordano (1985-1989), Executive Director, White House Watch, project of United States Public Policy Council.

Special thanks to the following who have made the publication of this review possible:

Senior Editor: Owen Jones

Executive Editor: Hanover Henry

Cover design and typesetting: Spencer Grahl

Legal Counsel: Amanda G. Hyland, Esq.

Taylor, English, Duma LLP, Atlanta, Georgia

This publication was made possible thanks to a grant from the Freedom Center Foundation.

Library of Congress Control Number: 2024931066

This pocketbook and the organizations which have worked together to publish and circulate it do not advocate for or against candidates for local, state or federal office or for or against any political party.

Donations to pay for more copies of this pocketbook to be printed and distributed may be made to:

White House Watch

A project of United States Public Policy Council, a 501/c/4 public policy corporation. Donations not tax deductible.

WhiteHouse.watch

or mail

White House Watch
Freedom Center, P.O. Box 820
Stuarts Draft, VA 24477-0820.

or

Freedom Center Foundation
Chairman@FreedomCenterFoundation.org

Gifts to the Foundation are tax deductible on your federal tax return. Gifts of $1000 or more are requested.
Recognized by IRS as a 501(c)3 charity.

Additional copies of this pocketbook may be ordered for a gift of $5 each, 3 for $10, 10 for $20, 100 for $150 plus postage and handling of $3 plus 10% of the cost of the pocketbooks. Inquire for larger orders.

FreedomPublishers.com for online orders & other books and pocketbooks.

Praise for Mark Levin's *The Democrat Party Hates America* and this book review

I fought the Marxists in Vietnam. It is unthinkable that they are running our government today. Mark Levin proves it. Read his new book.

Lt. Col. Dennis Gillem, USA (Ret.), chairman, Veterans Advisory Board of Uniformed Services League

I know senior citizens have been confused about all this hatred directed at them because they too, want to "Make America Great Again." Mark Levin explains why "The Democrats Hate America." They're Marxists.

Ronald Wilcox, Executive Director, Secure America Alliance

The Democrats are not pro-Marxist. They **are** Marxist. They espouse Marxist beliefs, use Marxist tactics. Use this paperback to tell everyone you know.

Emy Delgaudio, Chairman, White House Watch

The Communists support their own, as I wrote in 1980 in *China Doll: Clinton-Gore and the Selling of the Presidency*. They still are. Mark Levin's new book shows why.

Dr. Roger Canfield, Executive Vice President, United States Intelligence Council

Continued Page 6

Introduction

By State Representative Mike Jones
(R-York County PA)

Do you recall, June 2015 when he declared for President? The laughter stopped and the hate campaign against Donald Trump started shortly after, when the liberal-left realized he might win. It has continued non-stop for nine years.

Mark Levin's book, *The Democrat Party Hates America*, shows why leftwing Democrats hate Donald Trump and his followers. Because they hate America. Our founders. Our freedom. Our Constitution and its Bill of Rights with its restrictions on their power. All this hate, because they are Marxists.

If you read this with an open mind you will join me in saying "thank goodness there's finally a book that shows how Marxists have taken over the Democrat Party.

If this worries you: (1) buy the full-size book. (2) Send for more of this paperback to give everyone you know. (3) Donate to help distribute more paperbacks and promote the full-size book. The haters may prevail, if you won't.

It is time to work together this year to help Donald Trump "Make America Great Again." Let's thwart the Marxist Democrats.

Praise for Mark Levin's *The Democrat Party Hates America* and this book review *(continued from pg.4)*

Donald Trump and his "Make America Great Again" theme is about love and caring. In contrast, the Democrat Party is now all about hate. Mark Levin's book shows the choice for Americans in 2024 loving freedom, or hateful Marxism.

Kevin Peterson, National Project Director, Conservative Christian Center

The implication of Marxist-Democrat functionaries recruiting and training our military is mind-boggling. Mark Levin sounds the warning. I pray Americans will heed it.

Richard Buck, National Project Director, Uniformed Services League

1.
The Marxists are Winning in America

Mark Levin's new book, *The Democrat Party Hates America*, pulls no punches. He is, as his fans will recognize, direct and hard-hitting.

When the historical annals of this period of American history are written, after the patriotic and spiritual revival that conservatives hope will defeat the Marxist, Democrat Party's war on America, Mark Levin will be noted as one of its most courageous and decisive foot soldiers. After reading this review, and his new book—which we highly recommend—you will harbor no doubts that the Democrat party is now a Marxist party whose goal is to destroy the America of our Founding Fathers and leave our Founders in the eyes of future generations as hated symbols.

Truly, Mark Levin is right: the Democrat Party hates America and is waging relentless psychological warfare against everything that freedom-loving, God-fearing Americans hold dear. Their goal is not only to foment hatred of America and our founders, but their vitriol is aimed at those who do not agree with them. At the very least, that's half of America or, if you believe recent public opinion polls, more.

You will find Levin's overwhelming and unassailable facts and arguments to be a bit daunting. Perhaps more accurately, Levin paints a dismal future for America, given what the Marxist Democrats have been doing and the success their relentless hate campaign has enjoyed in recent years. You must have the courage to read and learn, as disturbing as these facts are.

Stopping the relentless Marxist juggernaut – those who today control the Democrat Party and many or most of the organs which influence public perception in America--is not going to be easy. We may suffer losses and disappointments in the short term. But we must be relentless and remember the simple call of Winston Churchill during the darkest hours of World War II: "never give in."

This requires a willingness to sacrifice on our part, just like the courageous airline pilots, military personnel, police and firemen and doctors and nurses who refused to yield to covid "vaccine" mandates. They were fired. But they are speaking out and filing lawsuits. We are beginning to see good, positive results as the result of their courageous efforts after two years of darkness for them and for those of us praying for them.

The truth doesn't always win in this world nor is the darkness always defeated. At least, not at first. Remember Christ Crucified but then the glory of Easter Sunday. This is a core belief of all orthodox Christians. Good sometimes (or perhaps often) only prevails when we are willing to sacrifice for our beliefs and convictions. We may lose people who we thought were our friends. We may even lose the approval of family members. But like Levin, we must become relentless in our defense of principles, and relentless in exposing the evil ideas and methods of the Marxist Democrats. Otherwise, we are doomed to being prisoners of the societal GULAG the Marxist Democrats have in store for us. If you are not fully persuaded yet, I hope you will read this review, and, better yet, buy and read the book.

2.
The Marxist War on the Family

This is a book review, not a summary. But the most important chapter of Mark Levin's book, "The War on the Family," deserves a closer look. It alone is well worth the price of the book, which we highly recommend.

Levin rightly reminds us that Marxism is not just an economic system designed to steal all of the wealth and property from the rich and distribute it to the poor, thus, theoretically, creating a classless society. The *Communist Manifesto's* most important agenda is to steal children from their parents and make them the property of the Communist State.

For the Marxists—as with their ideological cousins the Fascists of Italy and Germany of World War II—it is not just a slogan to say "youth are the future." It is their major, intergenerational strategy to seize the future by stealing the children of the present. They have worked on this for decades, for more than an entire generation in America.

Why is this so important? The Marxist Democrat Party wants to own your children, and they know they cannot accomplish their stated task of bringing about a "fundamental transformation of America" as long as a vibrant, healthy, nuclear family still functions.

All of their Marxist plans depend on the destruction of the family, defined as a mother and a father with children.

The family has been defined as the most

"reactionary" institution in human history. That's because mothers and fathers of children tend not to engage in revolutionary action. They want freedom, opportunity, prosperity, and moral guidance for their children and stability, not revolutionary change. As Levin points out, this urge is so strong that even Karl Marx himself--the primary advocate for the destruction of the nuclear family—could not overcome it. He doted on his own children, was generous toward them, and made provisions for their welfare by appointing Frederich Engels to be their guardian in the event of his death. If he were true to his ideology, he would have turned the care of his children over to the Communist Party.

Levin quotes one of the most important passages from the *The Communist Manifesto*:

"Abolition of the family! Even the most radical flare-up at this infamous proposal of the Communists. On what foundation is the present family, the bourgeois family based?

On capital, on private gain. In its completely developed form, this family exists among the bourgeois. But this state of things finds its complement in the practical absence of the family among the proletarians, and in public prostitution. The bourgeois family will vanish with the vanishing of capital. Do you charge us with wanting to stop the exploitation of children by their parents? To this crime we plead guilty. But, you will say, we destroy the most hallowed of relations when we replace home education by social."

Marx clearly believed that parenting is an act of exploitation. Today's American Marxist Democrats agree with him. Levin follows with case after case of policies by the Democrat Party to implement Marx's plan to abolish the family. "The good news for the Democrats," says Levin, "is that the number of unmarried women is growing every year. From the earliest census up through 1950, roughly 80% households were led by a married couple. By

2000, that percentage had fallen to 52%, and by 2010, for the first time in the nation's history, most households did not include a married couple. Marriage has only continued to decline since then. The destruction of the nuclear family may be great for Democrats, but it has been a disaster for children. The Democrat Party benefits hugely from the vote of unmarried women, and does poorly with married women." In the last Presidential election, "CNN exit polls found that 68% of unmarried women voted for the Democrats," Levin writes.

We can only imagine how much worse it will be, psychologically, morally and spiritually, for children raised by same sex parents! Not to mention how many of these damaged children will vote Democrat when they reach adulthood. That's the plan!

This explains why "Biden transitioned from a so-called moderate on the issue of abortion to the most radical president ever on the subject," says Levin. Biden's radical

Marxist Attorney General Merrick Garland has declared war on the American family. "He issued a memorandum threatening parents with FBI investigations should complaints be made against them by school administrators, teachers or anyone else. Garland's memo was addressed to the FBI, United States Attorneys, the Department of Justice's Criminal Division, the Civil Rights Division, and counter terrorism offices. It also encouraged complainants to use the domestic terrorism hotline to make their allegations."

And why would he brand parents as domestic terrorists? Levin summarizes as follows: "For insisting at school board meetings on the right to be heard, for exposing pornographic materials used in classrooms and libraries to promote the LGBT agenda, for the right to access curriculum materials, for the right to see school budgets and spending, for the right to protect their child's privacy, for the right to know about any violent threats at school."

Public school administrators and teachers are now insisting on promoting sex transition among pre-pubescent children, encouraging them to cross-dress on campus, while keeping this information from parents, according to Levin.

Levin reminds us that most pre-adolescent and adolescent children struggle with forming their own identity in the world, especially given the narcissistic and nihilistic cultural environment. However, there is significant expert opinion and scientific research, according to Levin, that the much touted "gender dysphoria" is typically a transitory stage in personality development. But the Department of Health and Human Services believes that every child questioning his identity must be given "gender-affirming care," which means encouraging them to take active steps to change their sex, including radical sex change surgery, without consulting their parents. This will all be paid for with your tax dollars of course!

One of the most disturbing conclusions to be drawn from Levin's research is that corporate America is a major driving force behind the sinister and, frankly, demonic policies that are anti-children and anti-family, with the Target Corporation being one of the worst offenders. For years, Target has partnered with a radical organization GLSEN (Gay, Lesbian, Straight Education Network), to not only promote the LBGT agenda in schools, but to actively promote and support sex changes for children. Target initially banned Levin's book from its stores, and only relented after public pressure.

Part of GLSEN's stated objective is as follows: "Staff or educators shall not disclose any information that may reveal a student's gender identity to others, including parents or guardian... This disclosure must be discussed with the student, prior to any action."

Since publication of this book, Target has come under public scrutiny and pressure after placing pro-LGBT and outright satanic messaging on its children's clothing line, in the most public displays as you enter their stores. But there is no evidence that they have substantially changed course in their support of anti-family policies. An increasing number of conservatives have made the decision to never again set foot in a Target store.

At the beginning of Covid, many well-meaning people went along with the draconian public policies that were supposedly intended to "flatten the curve" and save lives. But from the very beginning we knew that Covid did not pose a threat to children. And yet the teachers' unions and blue state governors especially conspired to close schools. And when they reopened, children were forced to maintain "social distancing" and to wear masks when no scientific evidence was put forward to justify these policies.

The data is now coming in. Children were severely harmed psychologically, and their educational progress was held back by these mandates. To speak up at school board meetings to question these mandates was to be branded as a Covid "denier" or worse, "and possibly subjected to the police powers of Biden's Department of Justice," according to Levin.

"Moreover, many scientists, researchers, medical professionals, statisticians, and even writers and broadcasters who did speak out in real time, raising legitimate and substantive questions about the federal government's dictates and blue state governors' actions, experienced threats, torment, denunciation and even had their careers ruined and licenses revoked. The Democrat Party media, social media sites, and others did all they could to ignore them or, worse, disgrace and silence them. And the Biden administration, working with Twitter and others, played a significant role in monitoring and censoring them," Levin writes.

Why? Because the State is sending you a

message: *We own your children. Don't question us or we will destroy you*.

Nowhere has this deliberate state takeover of the family seen more disastrous effects than among the black population of America. In 2005, "72 percent of black children...were born to unmarried mothers." "There is abundant evidence that boys growing up in these conditions have less self-control than those growing up in more stable families...and most of all, ...those boys are far more prone to commit crime," Levin writes.

The Marxist Democrats war against the black family, beginning with the so-called "Great Society," seems to have largely succeeded. But in fact, there is a stunning difference between the success of the black nuclear family and broken black families. An associate of mine recently told a black woman friend about the Thanksgiving dinner his wife and he had put on for 23 family members at their home. She replied that her family needed to hire a venue! If you have traveled our nation recently, you will frequently encounter black family reunions that needed to book several floors of a motel to accommodate everyone! They print up t-shirts celebrating this annual event. Yet black voters continue to vote against their best interests by throwing their political support overwhelmingly for the Marxist Democrats. Hopefully this will change soon, and black voters who have maintained the nuclear family structure will follow the recent trend of Hispanics to vote Republican. But for this to happen, we need to reach out to them!

3.

The Democrats are Totalitarian Marxists.

Levin points out that in Marxism, the Communist Party and the State are one.

That sure sounds like the Chinese Communist Party of today, which is to say, Red China the country. The Party and the

Country are one and the same.

Levin's central thesis in this book is not merely that the Democrat Party hates America, but that they operate the same as the Communists who control Red China and the Fascist Party which controlled World War II Germany and Italy. The Democrat Party, he argues, strives to create a one-party state in which every deceitful, illegal and unconstitutional method possible is used to prevent a Republican from ever again being elected President, of ever having the majority of the Supreme Court and Congress. They aim to have complete control of all levels of government in America. This is the essence of the Marxist ideology which is totalitarian to its very roots.

In order to achieve one-party control, they give drivers licenses to illegal immigrants and encourage them to use those drivers licenses to vote, even if they do not yet have the votes to turn 40 million illegal aliens into citizens. According to Levin, they give more welfare benefits and legal protections to illegal immigrants than to legal immigrants or American citizens. They have opened our borders and put out the word: "Welcome to America!," knowing that the vast majority of these illegals, when they are permitted to vote, will vote Democrat because they have no knowledge of America's history of freedom.

This also explains why the Marxist Democrats have embraced the shocking, perverse LGBT agenda. And it explains why Joe Biden, once a Democrat who aligned himself against civil rights for blacks and against the radical LGBT agenda, has fully embraced the Marxist agenda: he is drunk with power. Although it is most likely the influence of his handlers, since, as Levin points out, Biden is suffering from stage 5 of the well-established 7 stages of dementia.

As Levin explains, the focus on LGBT and on "Critical Race theory" attacks on white

America in supposed defense of oppressed blacks, is simple: they are creating divisions in America, hatred for what this country has stood for, with the goal of creating a new majority.

This campaign of hatred is the trademark of Marxists so it is hardly surprising that it is the major "philosophy" of today's Marxist Democrats.

The Marxist Democrats are shocked and dismayed that Donald Trump is capturing 40% of the Hispanic vote and an increasing number of black voters. This goes against their narrative that Americans, and MAGA Republicans specifically, are racist bigots who hate brown people and want to oppress them. Most Hispanics are pro-family. Many of them are pro-life Catholics who actually go to church and send their children to Catholic schools. They are beginning to realize that the Marxist Democrats hate them too for their hard work ethic and the fact that they are raising children and going to church. They must find a new generation of pro-Democrat Hispanic illegals to counter this significant Hispanic voting trend towards the Republicans. Were it not for two rogue Democrat Senators voting against their amnesty plan for illegal immigrants, the game might even be over already.

The Marxist Democrat Party hates the Constitution, and especially the First Amendment which guarantees free speech and religious liberty. Levin quotes the CEO for First Liberty Institute, who wrote: "for the first almost 100 years of our republic, there were *zero* cases decided by the U.S. Supreme Court concerning the Free Exercise [of religion] Clause of the First Amendment, and...then not another case for another 41 *years* after that." But beginning in 1940, "litigation on religious liberty has exploded at an alarming rate...." With 75 more cases!

The Biden Department of Justice has declared war on Christians, sending agents to infiltrate traditionalist churches. An FBI whistleblower says these cases are justified by accusing traditionalist Christians of being "ethnically motivated violent extremists," Levin reports.

The war on free speech under the Biden White House includes censoring conservative opinion as "disinformation." Levin extensively documents the conspiratorial nexus between the FBI and social media outlets such as Facebook and Twitter to sensor anyone who would question covid mandates, or who would dare dissent from Marxist orthodoxy, including 10 conservative media outlets, according to Levin. To take one example, PJMedia, which is a reliable source of political news and commentary on the conservative side of the spectrum, is completely deplatformed by most social media and deprived of hundreds of thousands of dollars in revenue.

Levin's book details how the Marxist Democrats seek total control over every aspect of society and the destruction of any force which might stop them. It is the essence of today's Democrat Party. It explains why they hate America, and why they will say and do anything to seize final, monopoly power which they will never let go of.

4.

The Party of Freedom

We who are freedom loving patriots have been scolded and warned for decades that our side is demographically destined to disappear. We are older, there are fewer and fewer white people as a percentage of the population (as if the Republican Party in general and conservatives especially are "white supremacists!), and we are doing nothing but standing in the way of progress.

This kind of talk by Marxist Democrats is racist and un-American as well as untrue.

Perhaps you have noticed already, but in

many ways the demographics of the two parties in America have inverted in recent decades, according to Levin. "Despite its 'get the rich' and Marxist class warfare propaganda, the Democrat Party has abandoned the working class—as most Marxist-centered movements have and do," Levin writes. "Nine of the top 10 wealthiest congressional districts are represented by Democrats, while Republicans now represent most of the poorer half of the country... The last several decades have ushered in a dramatic political realignment, as the GOP has broadened its base to a more diverse working class and Democrats have become the party of wealthier, more-educated voters."

The GOP has nothing but great potential to add black voters to its pro-family, pro-freedom agenda. And as Mark Levin also documents, it was "the Democrat Party who lynched blacks and had parties to celebrate while they were doing it, to stop them from voting and to suppress their influence after the Democrats lost the civil war fought to keep their slaves." It was the Democrats which launched the Klu Klux Klan to fight on in suppressing blacks and which opposed civil rights laws to protect black voters. Levin reminds us that a larger percentage of GOP Senators and Congressman voted for the 1960's civil rights laws than did Democrats. He reminds us as well that it was Joe Biden who told us that integration would lead to "a racial jungle."

The Marxist Democrat party advocates, supports, and in some cases dictates resegregation of racial and ethnic groups. To take one example, that Levin quotes: the District of Columbia Public School system is "developing racially segregated 'affinity groups'...to dismantle white supremacy, strengthen intersectional movements and advance the human rights of all people." This initiative is being pushed by the Southern Poverty Law Center, a radical Marxist lawyers group, which asserts that segregated groups aren't really "separatist and racist and that there is no need for whites to participate, other than if they wish to focus on support for students of color."

Republicans, and especially MAGA Republicans, should never yield an inch on the issue of civil rights. But too many cower in fear when they are labeled as racist.

Black Americans will rally around the GOP in large numbers if we campaign more assertively for school choice. This has been proven in state and local races around the country.

5.

MAGA vs Hate-Trump

The major "issue" of President Biden and his Marxist Democrats is hatred of President Trump and his "Make America Great Again" (MAGA) cause. It isn't working, except to motivate a shrinking minority of voters.

They know that he cannot be controlled and is the biggest impediment to their success. They will not stop in their efforts to destroy him, even if he wins election and if they cannot stop him from taking office.

For example, Trump was charged under The Espionage Act for the mishandling of his Presidential documents, and not, explains Levin, under the governing statute which is the Presidential Records Act. The Espionage Act, according to Levin, was signed into law in 1917 by liberal darling, President Woodrow Wilson, and is broadly written to provide Wilson with an excuse to jail 10,000 of his political opponents because of their criticism of him and his policies. It has never been used since. Not even when Jane Fonda was manning an anti-aircraft battery in North Vietnam and making hateful, pro-Communist, anti-America statements!

According to Levin, when Judicial Watch tried to obtain certain presidential records from the Clinton White House under the Freedom of Information Act, a left-wing, Obama-appointed federal judge shot it down. She determined that "Since the President is completely entrusted with the management and even the disposal of Presidential records during his time in office, it would be difficult for this Court to conclude that Congress intended that he would have less authority to do what he pleases with what he considers to be his personal records," Levin quotes.

"The judge noted a president could destroy any record he wanted during his tenure and his only responsibility was to inform the Archives," writes Levin. And yet, President Trump has been prosecuted under an entirely different law that is not-applicable, as if he were passing Presidential records to our enemies! The hypocrisy would be stunning, if we weren't already aware that this is a well-establish tactic of Marxists everywhere.

"Stalin Would Be Proud" is the title of

the last chapter of the book, in which Levin details the illegal and unconstitutional criminal charges against President Trump. "The Democrat Party's scorched earth, unscrupulous, and unconscionable political and criminal persecution of Donald Trump is totalitarian in every respect," Levin writes. "Joseph Stalin and his henchman, Levrentiy Beria, would be proud."

6.

Can Marxist Democrats be Defeated in November, 2024?

Under the demented Biden, the Democrat Party is imploding. Gone is their confidence of just a year ago, that the Republicans didn't stand a chance of electing a president. They are desperate, panicking. Having accused every white person in America of being a pro-slavery, white supremacists, and all Trump voters of being extremist, domestic terrorists, they have overplayed their hand. Natural forces are at work. Contrary to the liberal-left teachings, an increasing percentage of young people want to marry and have children. Roe v. Wade has been overturned, leading to extreme pro-abortion hysteria by the Democrats, something they always believed in but were afraid to make public. They actually have gone beyond late term abortion advocacy to seeking abortion up to the actual birth of a child. Only one Democrat in the House of Representatives voted for a bill to protect babies born alive after a botched abortion!

While both Trump and Biden have high unfavorable ratings, Trump is more popular than ever, and Biden's approval rating is the lowest of any president at this point in his first term. The legal persecution of Donald Trump is only making him more popular. The issues of Donald Trump and "Make America Great Again" Republicans, are increasingly popular with Americans, while Biden and his Party stick to their "hate MAGA" platform.

While establishment Republicans still control the GOP in Congress and the Republican National Committee, there is a growing grass roots rebellion. There is a massive downturn in fundraising for the GOP party machine. This is giving a huge advantage to Democrat candidates for office but, with those GOP candidates who have stood strong for the issues of interest to Trump-MAGA conservative Republicans, they have overcome that advantage to win their election contest.

And there are rising stars among the MAGA movement who give us hope for the future, such as Senators J.D. Vance (Ohio), Ted Cruz (Texas) and Mike Lee (Utah) and Congressmen such as Jim Jordan, Matt Gaetz and Scott Perry. The GOP may still be top heavy with RINO and establishment types but there is no question that they have more rising stars willing to speak out against the Marxist Democrats.

The Republicans are more likely to patch up their differences in 2024 than the Democrats. Democrat leaders increasingly fear a Biden defeat and are making public noises about replacing him as the nominee. But if Biden is forced out, they must nominate the verbally incontinent Vice President Kamala Harris or face a severe backlash from the Marxists who control the Democrat Party. Moreover, if Gavin Newsom were to be the nominee, the Democrat Party is at risk of losing what's left of its support among the working class and middle America.

Then there is the God question. The Marxist Democrats hate God and want to replace Him with their own power to bring about "the fundamental transformation" of America. The best defense against tyranny is to place our faith and trust in God, to obey His commandments, to stand up and speak out, to never apologize for what we believe, and never, never back down.

The values of middle America are the opposite of the Marxist-Democrats. If the great majority of traditional, patriotic, church-going Americans figure this out then the party of President Joe Biden is going to suffer a major defeat on election day, November 2024, and also lose control of the U.S. Senate, and watch conservative Republicans dramatically increase their majority in the U.S. House of Representatives from their narrow margin of today.

The only way to stop the Marxist Democrats who hate America so much from continuing their destruction of the land of freedom as Mark Levin reports, is for them to lose consecutive elections by wide margins. America will not be safe until the Marxists are totally on the run and no longer a clear and present danger to the survival of America. The Declaration of Independence, the Constitution and its Bill of Rights restrictions on government power, are the very antithesis of the Marxist Democrats aim for monopoly, totalitarian control of America.

Many of our voters, including those who did not vote for Joe Biden in 2020 and don't plan to vote for him or his party in 2024, forgot a very important point. For the Marxist Democrats, just like other Marxists, their guiding philosophy is their hatred of their opponents and their wish to destroy them completely. That means you, Dear Reader.

Mark Levin's *The Democrat Party Hates America* seeks nothing less than the total extermination of the Marxist influence and control of the Democrat Party and an end to their very serious threat to make America a one-party state forever.

Patriots who love America and what it has stood for, and who want to stop Marxists from seizing total control forever, should buy the Levin book, and hand out as many copies of this paperback as they can to help promote his ideas during 2024. Because our country's survival depends on you as never before.

About State Representative Mike Jones (R-York County PA)

Mike Jones excelled athletically and academically and was President of his senior high school class. After a full scholarship to DeVry University in Columbus, OH, he graduated first in his class.

In 2006 Mike was named president of St. Onge, an international supply chain strategy and logistics consulting firm until his retirement in 2017. Under his leadership, the firm was named one of the world's top 100 supply chain partners seven times and was named to Inc. Magazine's 5000 Fastest Growing Private Companies in the country each of the three years prior to his retirement.

Mike earned an "A" rating from Conservative Christian Center, associated with the publisher of this book, White House Watch, in his first run for State Representative in York, PA. He won that election and two more.

Mike has been an outstanding conservative, one of the strong supporters of President Trump from the start. Because he helped campaign for and defeat two powerful GOP State Legislators in York County, replacing them with stellar conservatives, the GOP retaliated by removing him from all Committee assignments.

Mike Jones is a founding member and first chairman of the PA House Economic Growth Caucus and a founding member of the PA State Freedom Caucus. He is the father of four children, all adopted from Russia.

About Former State Rep. Gary Giordano

Gary Giordano, Executive Director of White House Watch (formerly White House Defense Fund under President Trump), is a former State Representative in Arizona (1985–1989), married with 5 children and 6 grandchildren and a licensed Arizona Hunting guide, registered Representative and Insurance Agent.

Gary Giordano is a lifetime conservative, starting with Young Americans for Freedom as a chapter, regional and state chairman before being appointed to the National HQ Staff. He is a founding member of the independent YAF Archive, the Listserv for and by YAF senior alumni.

They laughed when he first ran for President.

But when they saw Donald Trump could win—and did—they started a nine-years long campaign of hate.

His most hard-hitting book yet, this review of Mark Levin's *The Democrat Party Hates America*, should be shared with all open-minded voters before the 2024 election.

Levin says the Democrat Party isn't just *sympathetic* to Marxism. They *are* Marxists. They hate Trump and you his supporters, because they hate America and freedom.

If the Democrat Party wins in 2024, it could very well be the last free election in America.

Help warn people. Read Levin's book. Distribute this paperback Review. Get the word out.

How to Order:

1 copy = $5 — 3 copies = $10

10 copies = $25 — 100 copies = $150

Please include a postage and handling fee of $3 plus 10% and make your check payable to and mail to:

White House Watch
Freedom Center Fulfillment Dept.
P.O. Box 820, Stuarts Draft, Virginia 24477-0820
Or **www.whitehouse.watch**

Don't miss your chance to own the new publication with the power to crush socialism in America—a conservative must-have for the Biden era!

It's a fact: right now, **socialism is winning**, and **conservatism is losing**. But this new paperback, *A Review of the Book United States of Socialism by Dinesh D'Souza,* helps conservatives rally everyday Americans against Biden-backed Marxism and preserve the founding principles of our country.

Not only does this paperback equip you with all the arguments you need to expose your friends, relatives, and co-workers to the evil truths of socialism, but, even better, you can order extra copies and gift them to open-minded Americans, so they too join the fight to ensure our Republic withstands the Biden era and elect "America First" conservatives in 2024!

How to Order:

1 copy = $5 | 3 copies = $10
10 copies = $25 | 100 copies = $150

Please include a postage and handling fee of $3 plus 10% and make your check payable to and mail to:

White House Watch
Freedom Center Fulfillment Dept.
P.O. Box 820, Stuarts Draft, Virginia 24477-0820
Or **www.whitehouse.watch**

They laughed when I said no, Donald Trump was not responsible for the COVID-19 virus. But when I gave them this little paperback…

Liberals desperately want Americans to believe Donald Trump was responsible for COVID-19. They want Joe Biden to get the credit for Donald Trump's successful vaccine rollout, and, more than anything, they want to stop a Trump comeback in 2024.

But this paperback exposes their **Big Lies** and tells the truth about how Donald Trump saved millions of lives.

This paperback will give you the facts you need to wipe the smirks off the faces of the Liberals who blame Donald Trump for COVID-19. Or take it a step further and help us share the truth with open-minded Americans to stop the spread of their Big Lies.

How to Order:

1 copy = $5 3 copies = $10
10 copies = $25 100 copies = $150

Please include a postage and handling fee of $3 plus 10% and make your check payable to and mail to:

White House Watch
Freedom Center Fulfillment Dept.
P.O. Box 820, Stuarts Draft, Virginia 24477-0820
Or **www.whitehouse.watch**

About White House Watch

A project of United States Public Policy Council

White House Watch has fought to combat the corruption, incompetence, and socialist policies of Joe Biden's government and before that, to defend (previously as White House Defense Fund) liberal-left attacks on President Trump. White House Watch accomplishments (partial list):

- ✓ Had one of only two amicus curiae (or "friend of them court") legal briefs accepted by the US Supreme Court challenging the irregularities in the 2020 presidential election. The Constitution – we argued – gives sole power to change the "time, manner and place" of elections to state legislatures not the Democrat Governor or city mayors. Justice Clarence Thomas agreed with WHW's argument in his written legal opinion. Had we prevailed, it would have invalidated the "election" of Joe Biden.
- ✓ Delivered a record-breaking quarter million signed petitions to Congress demanding the expulsion of Joe Biden allies Nancy Pelosi and Adam Schiff. This helped lead to the defeat of nine Democrat Pelosi-puppet Congressmen and the loss of the Democrat Majority!
- ✓ Launched a (partially) successful nationwide petition drive urging the appointment of a Special Prosecutor to investigate the Biden Crime Family – including the President himself – for suspicious and millions of dollars paid to his family and him linked to Red China and other U.S. adversaries.
- ✓ Published 411,500 copies of "A Review of The United States of Socialism by Dinesh D'Souza," Review by our Executive Director.
- ✓ Published 408,648 copies of the paperback "Big Lies: How Trump Overcame Liberal Lies to Fight the China Virus."
- ✓ Arranged a meeting of our Executive Vice President with President Trump, who thanked him for our financial support of the ongoing Trump "Freedom Tour."
- ✓ Most recently filed another Amicus Curiae Legal Brief with the Supreme Court challenging the role of local courts in drawing district lines for Congressmen and State Legislators, which – we argue – is the sole province of the State Legislatures per the Constitution (exactly echoing our argument in our earlier Supreme Court brief).
- ✓ Filed a successful complaint against Hillary Clinton for illegally "laundering" campaign funds to create the "Steele Dossier" used to justify FBI spying on the Trump campaign. She (her campaign and the Democratic National Committee) was forced to pay a $107,000 fine by the Federal Election Commission as a result of the White House Watch complaint (it took 3+ years).
- ✓ Published 62,000 "Summary of By the People? The 2020 U.S. Presidential Election and Theft of Americans' Right to Self-Rule," by Dr. Dan Brubaker, intro by Former State Rep. Gary Giordano, White House Watch Executive Director.

The work of White House Watch is paid for by the gifts of our supporters.